Let Us Leave Them Believing

Katie Campbell

Let Us Leave Them Believing

Methuen

Acknowledgement are made to the following publications
in which some of these poems first appeared:
*Acumen, Distaff, Descant, Foolscap, Grain, Iron,
Jennings, Kunapipi, Orbis, Outposts, Poet's Gallery,
Prairie Fire, Prospice, Queen's Quarterley, Rialto,
Room of One's Own, Slow Dancer, Struga International
Poetry Review 1988, Writing Women.*

'Eleven Fifteen, the Algonquin Hotel' was broadcast
on BBC radio as one of the winners of the 1986
National Poetry Competition.

'Blue' was included in *New Christian Poetry*,
ed. Alwyn Marriage (Collins/Flame 1990)

'Belugas' was included in *The Green Anthology*
ed. Robert Hall (Wayland Publishers 1991)

First published in Great Britain in 1991
by Methuen London, Michelin House,
81 Fulham Road, London SW3 6RB

ISBN 0 413 65030 8

A CIP Catalogue record for this book
is available from the British Library

Printed and bound in Great Britain
by Cox and Wyman Ltd, Reading

for J.

Contents

Eleven Fifteen,
The Algonquin Hotel

Eleven Fifteen, the Algonquin Hotel

So, you've made it –
a room with a bowl full of fruit
compliments of the management;
ten minutes into New York and we're fighting again
about something, nothing:
     what does it matter these days

till the telephone rings
blessedly bringing its meetings and conferences
people to see over lunches and dinners
and drinks in the evening
(generally wives are included in these).

You hang up the phone, distractedly gather your papers
'We'll finish the argument later,' you say
knowing, as I do, we won't;
not that there's anything left to be said anyway.

Maybe I'll see you dash past for a shower
snatched between meetings
(outside it's a hundred and three)
or maybe for breakfast
behind the papers, before the calls begin

maybe we'll smile surreptitiously
over a table of clients, or friends we both hate
begging off early, explaining
'Although it's not late he has to be up before dawn.'

Then back in the room you will, indeed, fall asleep
and I'll watch you, eyelids fluttering over your cheek
as you curl and roll over
away from me.

What would we have said anyway
on this evening, like so many others?
Together, alone, we are nothing;
we live in the public sphere
– you always did perform better in front of an audience.

What can I offer you: me, a memory of you
a fading impression of us – alone in this room
where the untouched fruit is beginning to rot.

red sky

I read somewhere
that in costa rica
perhaps in fact
throughout the tropics
– if costa rica is indeed in the tropics –
and even if it isn't

before the Big Storm
everything goes
awry
seasnakes
race inland
to suffocate
in surburban swimming pools,
insects bound
into the ocean
to drown and trees
twist green leaves upside-
down exposing
secret silver

last night I dreamed
of eating roses
with a man I knew
a while ago
– twelve days
to be precise –
yes I've reckoned
every minute
up . . .

it's time we talked
again

Ballad

I want to cradle your head like a stone
in the curve of my shoulder, the cup of my palm
in the pit of my gut where you left me alone
I want to cradle your head like a stone.

I want to cradle your head like a stone
to caress it soft, with a sculptress's hands
to bury it deep in the heat of the sands
to fling it far out in a smouldering sea
to smash it on rocks the way you smashed me
I want to cradle your head like a stone.

I want to cradle your head like a stone
to use it to bruise the flesh of my thighs
to gash at my groin, till the sigh of my cries
stops the moan of your groans
while I cradle your head like a stone.

I want to cradle your head like a stone
and swallow it whole.
                    I won't feel alive
till you slide down the tightrope of my insides
And I will consume you as you consumed me
and I will possess you, oh so tenderly
when the cradle you fill is the cage of my bones.
I want to cradle your head like a stone.

Bedtime Stories

I
it always rains
these nights when you're away

I count the drops that hit the pane
thinking of toast and other mundane things

wondering why you did
– or didn't – phone

and if I really could make it alone . . .

II
we apologize more than we make love these days
even when we're making love

we seem to have lost the desire
to laugh except at other peoples' jokes

III
in the dark the hours pass
twelve . . . one . . . two . . .
I mimic sleep, pretending not to mind
your absence in the many hiding places of this house

beneath the bed the cats hiss
spitting menace at each other
– this is how we will destroy our children:
not the facts, complaints proclaimed
but this low growl which undermines our life.

Urban Relations

I

I think
it was your shrink
who came between you and me;

or am I being dim
was it me
who came between you and him?

II
I'm having a secret affair
with my husband
our lovers don't know

you think I'm joking
keep 'em guessing
that's my motto

III
Someday it will come to you
late at night as you are lying with some woman
who may be your wife

when every thing is easy except sleep
you'll realize that you were wrong
to let me go.

Coming to Terms

It begins with a secret
you decide to keep
to yourself;

there is such strength in this
that you decide to keep
a second

secret . . . thus you seize
the power, despite your own
denials

you have grown too big
for the unit, it will never fit
again;

then there's just the slow
inexorable
coming to terms.

Pendulum

The moon has got stuck in its pendulum swing
suspended, one third of the way up the sky;
you want to release it

you know it won't matter
it's part of a pattern you don't understand
but you have a special affinity for things that are stuck.

You love him: you don't want to leave him.
You hate him
you love him, you don't want to leave him
although he has asked you to go.

You married for life, but it's over, he says;
can something still hurting
this much be called dead?

A break-down, a break-up, you give it a name
but the thing doesn't change –
like the moon

as you drive in the dark by the river
still perching, precarious
threatening to slide

right out of the sky.

Blue

Recently I've been thinking of blue
the blue of the mosque in Istanbul
and the Pudding Shop book
where we signed our names
looking for notes from people we knew who'd been
    there before
that night we split from the rest
and headed north again
hitching through rain
and the fine line between boredom and despair
till we got to Prague
– the flat you borrowed from a friend
(you said you didn't know it was only one room).

I've been thinking of blue, the river, the Danube?
pierced by St Vitus' wavering spire:
all the cathedrals in Europe that year
and this is the one I remember by name
the symmetry perfectly scaled to inflame;
I thought if there is a God, he is here
in this city with so many churches, and you a Jew
then you disappeared into the winding streets
of a language you didn't speak
looking for condoms . . . I grinned to myself
and counted one more hurdle (almost) cleared
in the obstacle course to maturity
until you returned with two ice-creams
so I learned about abstinence too.

Recently I've been thinking of blue
of your eyes when we put our foreheads together –
if there were a God I suppose he would have
impossibly blue eyes too.
Some days I long to climb inside
and rest along the crest of those lids
rocked while the waves of your breathing
slowly cover me over
till nothing remains
but the memory of you
and that summer in Prague.

Lullaby

(*for B.*)

Think of her as the Thames
the quick of it or the breath of it
and this is a long slow Saturday morning
she's taking you in her arms
away from the shadowy source
the thick lugubrious mud
the small thin trickle of life
slithering out of the earth
lulled in her loose embrace
and the current which knows where it's going
pushed by the hurrying waves
she's leading you down to the sea
out to the willow green sea
up to the sea blue sky.

Moorhens

They hatched today, like animated dustballs
crashing through the long grass
popping into the pond.

That afternoon, your twins
when we collected them from kindergarten
looked at me suspiciously;
they let me help them on with mitts and boots
but later one of them kicked the back of your seat
as you manoeuvred through the traffic:
'Mom, Mom,' he chattered, anxious
'That's not Mom,' the other one corrected him,
'that's Poppa's friend.'

The chicks cheep, troubled
round the pond
their mother not responding.

In the undergrowth a crow
or some dark bird
dips his beak

the cat stops licking herself
on the oven stone
beside the cottage:

there are so many hazards
one almost overlooks the magpie
waiting at the water's edge.

Magician

You licked the quick then split.
You conjured a possibility which wasn't,
but you did, then disappeared it.
You hypnotized the skipping ropes from two
knot-bound to one, which suddenly was found
to be not one but two.
You juggled with bubbles I'd long since thrown away
and magicked the night into a play
in which I was the leading lady
but the brightest star fades first
and everybody knows that magic's only in the mind
of the beholder:
for the magician it's just another trick.

Triolet

Was it just a simple seven year itch
something as empty as that?
I don't expect True Love – nothing so kitsch –
but was it all simply a middle-aged itch
for which you used me – a Romantic – that's rich
a discontent housewife – to scratch.
Was I simply your one last ditch seven year itch
was it really as banal as that?

The Key

Today I saw a key
gleaming between the dark rails of the Northern line
the deepest line in London
the worst, most dirty, slow
subject to floods and sudden
unexplained halts
just before or just after the station,
the line most likely to display the sign:
'Delay due to body under train.'

Perhaps the key –
an ordinary house key
lying amid the whispery things
which skitter through wrappers
and soft shadows of dust
perhaps the key was simply dropped
– by mistake.

Today it's finally, slowly fading;
the edges of this story
this shape of your face,
your eyes which gleamed, now whisper,
your body, which thundered over me
is dust.

Let Us Leave Them Believing

Let us pretend we are lovers again
just once for this visit
to friends who thought we were perfect together

for all the love and the envy
they wasted on you and me
let us leave them believing.

Some Mornings I Can Hear Them Singing

Honeymoon

A week of sunsprung conversation
Venice after all these years,
Venice as we vowed we'd see it:

sleeping under bridges
begging at the convent door
divesting our destinies on strangers,
strangers led us to this city of mirages:
Sienese madonnas (you)
– almond eyes cast down before the Saviour,
gypsy trios flirting melodies
past titillated ladies sipping lemon tea
late afternoon in the piazza (me).

One afternoon we scripted it: the honeymoon
with noses pressed against the jewels
rooms we didn't dare to enter
ideas to entertain . . .

Now we have returned,
our husbands left in loggias
we hoard the day – too much to say
in the confinement of a small café.

Two married women now
and after all these years
we still avoid the time or place
to ask each other Why.

We call this Life,
wheel out the small confessions
smothered by the private choices made so long ago;
we call this conversation Life
who are we kidding, this is Art.

Widows

Someday we'll be old together
share a life again at last
all the headlines and the deadlines
and the bylines will be in the past.

We'll spend our evenings rocking on a wide verandah
musing on our children, and the lives we did
or didn't lead, the greetings and departures
which marked our growing greed.

We'll spend our mornings making jam
our afternoons coaxing a small garden from the sand;
tickled by the spray of waves we'll walk along the sea
living out the ageing scenes we script
each time we meet
sighing for the dreams we fashion now,
which will be then
wondering what we'd change if we could do it all again.

We'll be hearty widows, easy in our peace
wry and stout with wisdom, living as we please.
We'll make the slow decline from desire to distraction
from cigarettes to pills.

Stoking ancient fires
knitting scarves against the cold
we will live forever in that future when we're old:
it's the passion now that kills.

Waiting

(Royal Academy, 12. 2.88)
for Teresa and Ruth

We wander through The Age of Chivalry:
full of busy, almond-eyed men,
secure in their faith in their place in the world
their faith that brought grain or acceptance of famine.

You wince and glance round for a seat —
the plinth of a 12th century ironwork gate:
sinewy swans curve through primitive forgings.

We're stopped by a guard
directed to benches in room number five.
'It's coming,' you murmur. Another false start.
You rise up, restless.

I love the annunciations:
the dove or the word or the angel
whispering into her ear.

'She didn't even get a fuck,' you twist in pain,
or anticipation of pain,
or simply the wretched weight of waiting.

A man seeing you stroking your belly
makes space by a battered, wooden St George
slaying a demurely conceding dragon.

Your eyes have that distant, pupil-less look
of worn-out madonnas
on church façades.

'There are no pregnant madonnas,' you say,
'can you think of a pregnant madonna?'
Then you wince again, and scurry to sit.

'This is it.' But it doesn't recur,
and we're pressed to give up our places
to two old ladies, tired, with less to anticipate.

'Let's go.' If it doesn't come today they'll induce it.
This time tomorrow, today will just be a story:
'The day before you were born . . .'

As we stroll back through the manuscript room
I notice on an intricate page
a tiny creature etched in gold

stepping, tentatively, out of the frame . . .

Rosary

'ye will know them by their grievances'

What do you think J?
We've done pretty well, I suppose;
we've managed this far pretty easily
when you consider . . .

Jean
with her abortion
performed out of town

& Joan
with her mystery illness
which no one will call a nervous breakdown

& Jane
whose mother's about to die:
the Big C, I think but no one will say

& June
whose man
just up and went away

& Jennifer? Jillian?
– something like that –
your friend who's now a whore

& Judith
onto her second child
with a man she doesn't know anymore

Our own little troubles: cystitis, the body's revenge
– moralistic Old Bitch that she is – are really quite small
    retribution.

But worry not: these murmurings
these tiny seeds of discontent
these petals rolled through anxious fingers
countless counters
sacred sores, these shibboleths

                    are but
                the beads of
              one lone woman's
              rosary, many more
          will follow these through
            out the decades, each
            ensconsed between
              the Paternosters
                and the
                        Glorias . . .

Aubade

Why do women betray each other?
I don't expect an answer
and this is not a poem
I just rang to say I miss you
I knew you'd be away
leaving the machine
to take my question

I don't expect an answer
it's just sometimes I still wonder
how we ended up with half the world between us
I was thinking of your wedding day
when you climbed in beside me
your arms around my waist
my back against your face

I felt your tears
I wondered if you knew
that I cried too
before you said
to me or the impending day
before you climbed back to your bed:
why do women betray each other?

Sisterhood

I wanted to thank you
for the mangoes on the beach
which you even peeled, so chivalrously
sweet, thick juice dripping on your salty skin
while I, too cold as ever, sat and watched you swim;

for the birthday cake with candles
which you arranged in the garden
while I lay back all morning brooding in the sun;

for the trip to Madam Petrolinga
– world renowned clairvoyant –
who said that I was young, had two kids
no career, adored my husband – all of which are false.
And added that I fancied other women's men.

I wanted to thank you for letting me drink all the wine
and cry all down your lover
then insisting that he drive me home.

I wanted to thank you
but instead I've stolen your best times:
(I still have his voice on the answerphone).

Obit

on Pier 29
her books and newly sharpened
pencils neatly stacked
beside the razor blades

she'd tried before to die
but not with such
precision

Marmalade

'It's the marmalade season,' my sister murmurs
shivering beside me in that place on 14th Street:
my first visit, her first year away.
'Mum'll be slicing the oranges now . . .'
Hard little suns; pithy, thick-skinned promises.

Tinsel from the stripped tree glitters in the early gloom,
This should be the month of beginnings
January in Manhattan;
it's too cold to move, too cold to stay put.
'She'll be measuring the sugar
stirring with her wooden spoon.'

                    Not too sweet, not in this family –
she's famous for her Bitter Orange Marmalade, our mum:
'Just enough sugar to keep it from souring,'
she makes it powerful: biting, but strong.

In County Mayo

We're greeted by Mrs O'Grady
making noises which you assure me are English
discreetly translating her speech into words;
she smiles that not-to-be-patronized smile
– after all she knows what I'm saying
it is *I* who can't understand *her*.

Beneath the neon Madonna
perched on the soundless TV
despite protestations she lays out sandwiches and tea
before we, giggling, make our escape
into her cottage with walls thick as cart tracks
to nowhere.

The fire is lit, there's milk in the fridge
and butter and bread, and cold, clean sheets.

Your husband, she said
before we retreated, your husband
– meaning you, when you'd gone for the bags –
your husband should be all right in that bed
it's short, but it's tough, she nodded
– like the rocks, like the sheep.

She knows about husbands she does:
her own, twenty years gone
leaving her two simple sons and an acre of scrub.
Oh yes, she knows about husbands
with her flickering Madonna
and her mute TV.

Madonna

Suddenly I came upon you
silent in your niche of stone
as children played below:

those eyes, which once inspired, exude only sadness
tired now from too much watching over
– that eternal female impotence:
you see disaster coming
warn unheeded, see it come to pass
all you can do is wait
then try to ease the aftermath.

The centuries have worn a scar of tears across your face
although you still appear to see
the petty, private tragedies
the deaths and births and deaths again
a secret witness to our lives
Mother to us all, to some
– to most a mother only to one man.

What comfort can you give today
from where you stand . . . eternal?
No I doubt it; even stone eventually is worn away.

Mother-in-Law

Emaciated, wide-eyed mask,
your face retreating
where your mind fought, desperate, not to follow,
all the lines still duly etched in lipstick and mascara
without the form beneath to give them meaning
    beyond vanity
and that courageous keeping-up-appearances
which pulled us through.

That final week we watched you
meeting out the family history:
first the jewels, then the stories
carefully presented for posterity,
and finally the apologies –
yours, there wasn't time for ours.

I just wanted to tell you
I always assumed that we'd become friends
when I gave birth to your grandchildren,
I thought the petty things would pass
with that new life composed
– bizarrely when you think of it –
of you and me; I didn't expect this death so soon.
At least we agreed on these last things. At last.

But explanations come too late.
Tragedy – not even tragedy – Death
brings out the lurking cliché.

What I wanted to say was
when all hope of life was dead
you taught us how to die.

On Learning of the Holocaust

she married a Jew
and practiced self denial:

ate one bowl of soup, one celery stick,
'You can never be too rich or too thin,' she'd quip
with a flick of her wrist, and a nod 'No thanks,' to more

dressed in whimsical second-hand clothes from Oxfam,
'Shopping's such a bore,' and boots with holes
hidden deep in the soles

saved envelopes and string
patted strays in alleyways
read messages on noticeboards

ran for hours in the rain
dreamed of perfectly empty
perfectly square white rooms

had nightmares about chocolate cake
and fantasies of annihilation.

She Sings for Him

The Singing Nun
committed suicide
leaving a lesbian lover.

'That's not quite how the papers put it:
'Overdose in flat shared
with a woman friend.'

Too late she noticed that old peacock fame;
by then he'd flown. Oh chickadee, oh morning dove
you should have remained in your holy cage.

once the door is open
once the bars are busted once
you can't return, you see it disappears

– the cage – and then there's nothing to believe in.
(I mean if you can't believe in The Singing Nun
what the hell can you believe in?)

For G. Who Lives Alone

You have become our Mother Confessor:

through urban nights we dream of you,
spartan in your cottage by the sea

we turn to you as to the ocean
mammoth in its constancy

and you the endless pebbled beach, wrecked by waves
incessantly, but always you emerge – a little lost

a little gained, a torn shell here
and there a bit of driftwood, a shimmer in the sand;

we come and go and leave you to your solitude,
but though we whisper to each other in our sleep

we keep our secrets just for you . . .

Ces Plaisirs

(Colette 1873–1954)

'These pleasures,' she wrote:
garlic stinking vagabond
ancient as the sphinx
winking feline nods at passing fancies

– strutting naked on the stage
in limelight, by shaded lamp
across the thick, blue pages

inscribing every glance and sigh
from blushing adolescent thighs
to silks supporting sagging flesh;

when desire's reduced to flaccid speculation
when even lust gives way to friendship
and even friends die off

the mushrooms still thrust
their gamey buttons through the earth
if you just know where to look –

These pleasures which we lightly call.
'These pleasures
which we lightly
call physical.'

Taking Stock

Thirty-one, feeling eighteen
still the envy of my friends

married love, not passion, affection, not desire
the church bells ring on Sundays

I always wanted to live near a church
some mornings I can hear them singing

I grow roses in my garden, I fill my house with roses
and dream of people eating me

men, a man, a child would do
Teresa, my breast aches

is this a cliché
my womb – my womb? the emptiness after sex

feels emptier than usual
I seem to spend the whole time on my own

when the cat disappeared I wanted to die
I still get a thrill each time my name's in print

each time the phone goes it's a possibility
cut off in the answering; I still attend the call

I love my (mostly absent) husband
I think I love my life

Teresa, smothered in domestic bliss
sometimes I still wonder

is this all
is this it . . .

Fraises des Bois

Fraises des Bois

We walk through the forget-me-nots, at first trying not to tread on them, then forgetting. What little imprint footprints make in meadows anyway. I'm telling you: 'This path, I used to gallop down it, over the field, into the sea.' You, not quite believing I could ever ride a horse in the spray. Me not quite believing it either. 'Round the corner,' I say, 'where the sand begins, will be a patch of fraises des bois: wild strawberries.' I pull back the brush, reveal them to you: secret stains flashing red. The tiny bites burst with summer.

Rain drips off the cedars edging the beach. Each step is a story. Me trying to convince you of a past that's gone, you smiling faintly, not really listening. When Grandad married his second wife, the cook gave them a bowl of fresh picked fraises des bois. What a perfect present everybody said. Then she quit.

Mrs Green. Every spring you'd see her in the forest, in the ditches, searching for new sources in the black flies and mosquitoes, in the pebbles and the thistles, in the long, snakey hay, in the spiky, yellow straw. In the heat of her kitchen hulling berries, dusting off dirt (if you wash them they go soft), measuring, stirring in sugar, boiling the jam on the hottest day of summer. *Confiture aux Fraises des Bois*: two hundred tiny jars this year, fifty more than last year. All proceeds to the hospital where her daughter died ten, twenty, thirty years before.

Rich as Croesus, she could simply have written a cheque. Nobody knew the effort. But there must have been some solace in it.

Remembering this particular site, on the edge of the woods, in the salt-rimmed sand, with headlands disappearing down the river, I planted wild strawberries in my London garden. 'Do they keep you awake with their revelry, your wild strawberries?' Dana asked. Dana has a strawberry birthmark on her left breast. At her request they left it when they took away the rest.

It doesn't come out, the red. It fades slower than all the other colours. Walking back after a christening one summer in late adolescence. Too much champagne and we ducked, me and some boy, off the path to search for berries. 'I know a secret place, I'll show you.' Benisons, from one to the other, cramming each other's mouths with handful after handful. These days I would do it one by one, savouring the sour surge. Kneeling into a patch in my most expensive skirt: a spurt of berry. It's still the brightest colour on the cloth. Yes I still can and do wear the skirt.

One year we had a laundress, half Indian, half French. She told us, rocking on her verandah when we'd come to deliver or retrieve, how when she was a child her mother kept the whole family alive on berries: wild strawberries, blueberries, blackberries, gooseberries.

They'd forage through from spring to autumn selling the berries to the English. So tiny, so low in the dust. To feed a family of eight and one drunken husband on so little. Wooden baskets dumping in a tin pail. Pink ping ping. Then as it gets fuller: plonk, plunk, plunk. And finally the dull, accepting silence of layer upon layer shifting to accommodate yet another layer.

The seeds are smaller than in cultivated berries, they grind deeper into the holes in your teeth. You can walk around for days worrying a trapped seed with your tongue or your finger.

When we were too young to refuse, Mum and Uncle several summers before he committed suicide, dragged us kids up to the sandy hills above the boulevard. It was private property. We were scared that it was stealing, but they said wild strawberries belonged to whoever tamed them. She must have been younger then than I am now. A lark for her and Uncle. Or maybe it was something they thought up to amuse us on a hot afternoon. They were on lookout. Duck! they'd shout when a car appeared and we'd scramble into the bushes and giggle.

It is years since I've been here early enough to catch the fraises des bois. Indeed I haven't been to this place at all since I left home. I don't think you understand how privileged you are. Fraises des bois are very rare: a luxury. They're especially fat this year because of all the rain.

We used to smash them on our cheeks like rouge. And on our lips. Make-up was vulgar, so we had to lick it off each other's faces before going in to tea.

One year I tasted white strawberries from the kitchen garden of a large estate. Like white chocolate they had less taste. 'I'd rather the real ones,' I said. By the time I heard how rude it was, the words were already out. The woman of the house smiled wanly; she'd already pegged me for a pleb.

Granny had a friend once – a very rich, very wrinkled, very vain, old woman, who used to paint a heart in the middle of her lips. Everybody laughed at her, but I thought it was lovely. She had the biggest garden on the boulevard and sometimes we were sent to pick her strawberries. You could do it almost standing up; you didn't need to crouch because they were so big. They didn't hurt your back so much. But they weren't as good to eat as fraises des bois.

My grandmother loved wild strawberries. She had a whole set of china imported from England with bright, red berries painted on each piece. When she died, and Grandad remarried, and the cook quit, they sold the house. I suppose that's when I grew up and left. I saw her soup tureen in the window of the antique shop this morning.

There is a Bergman film called *Wild Strawberries*. Everyone's heard of the film, everyone I know has seen it. But nobody can quite remember what it's about.

I'm trying to think of everything I know about wild strawberries.
I'm trying to tell you everything I know.
What I'm trying to say here is:
I know it's over but I haven't the strength to let go.

A Man in a
Foreign Hotel

Picnic at St Naum

(Poetry Festival: Struga, Yugoslavia)

Tables laid in willow shade,
casks of green wine flow like the River Drim
– meaning 'dream' –
licking at poets musing on Lowell and Hikmet:

these are philosophers,
words backed with freedom,
a tree which grows stronger the more it is pruned.

Erik confesses: 'My children
don't write, they want more security.
Yes, there were hardships, and yet, and yet . . .'

Yozo – eyes like flamingos,
choking: 'My wife is a hawk, her breasts
the bodies of flocks of dead sparrows.
Save me,' he pleads.

Yozo wants to dip, to suck, sliding, slow
down his throat, the silver skins, the smooth
fat weights, the ache in his belly stilled by fish after fish.

A willow bough flickers.
Erik, I could live here. 'There will be other days,'
he says, 'for you.' Taking my hand:
    'You know I'm a grandfather.'

Somewhere behind us the monastery stands,
on the edge of these waters of unmeasured depth,
cradling fish which haven't evolved in ten million years.

Maps

(*for Erik*)

That last night
while the stars burned out
as stars do every night around the world
and the coffees cooled, untouched, between us,
I wanted to trace the vein, pulsating
down your hand.

I have been thinking of that skein,
throbbing under your crepe thin skin
and of the star, which you supposed was Venus
though I disagreed – Venus being the evening star
I thought it was too late.
I was wrong.

Tonight the star still hangs above me,
still bright, still followed by a smaller, duller star
shielded in its shadow as it was on that last night.
Now I wish I'd done it –
traced the line of your thick vein
across your loosened fist and up your arm.
That's all. But I wish I had.

The Marketplace

Black wrapped women, sinister
in gap-toothed grins, behind red mountains of paprika
importune you.
Yozo tries to trick you into licking the spice:
'Taste it,' he twinkles, 'it sizzles.'
You know enough to resist.

Beyond the rows of open melons – drunken boats
for wasps gorged in an orgy of fermented syrup –
wrinkled men hawk wooden trinkets;
Yozo angles to buy you one: 'A present,' he grins,
'to remember me.' You settle
for a shared bag of grapes.

At the end of the stalls, where children play,
a tap drips into a stone trough.
Yozo suddenly concentrates,
washing his fruit, meticulous, till, thoroughly sluiced
he grips the stem, plucking the clusters one by one,
careful not to contaminate the shiny flesh with fingers
(you realize then, you are safe).

Owls

Back to back in the pillow padded den of
just before dawn on an ordinary day
an owl calls. Silence.

The ensuing shriek reminds you
of the cry you wrenched once
from a man in a foreign hotel

him gripping the headboard
hair curling, random, the mane of a centaur.
Suddenly you were galloping

tripping, slipping, suddenly
you were flaying this stranger;
you thrust your wrist

between his curled back lips
to stop his howls from hammering the wall
behind which other strangers listened.

And here, in your own bed
wedged against your chosen man
you wonder: why don't we bring each other such
        ecstasy?

Does it depend on strangers
or is it simply too dangerous to display
to the one you love?

Tonight They're Dancing on the Berlin Wall

(*9.11.89*)

Tonight they're dancing on the Berlin Wall.
You said that I looked worried in my sleep.
The bulldozers are joining in the squall.

We watch them, all those thousands, on TV
I find that I am struggling not to weep.
Tonight they're dancing on the Berlin Wall.

I'm terrified that someone's going to fall
they're stepping near the edges they can't see
the bulldozers are ramming at them all.

At least, tonight, they have the right to fall
off either face, although the street's embrace
is fatal still on both sides of the Wall.

It's easy, you say, just commit to me:
commit, submit, surrender – so I stall.
The bulldozers still bash on in their thrall.

The rubble spreads out in a dirty pall.
From this destruction will come unity
– you say – this smashing of the Berlin Wall.
The bulldozers are joining in the squall.

April in Paris

We meet for lunch at the Cluny Museum.
You start on the relativity theory:
how the observer affects the observed.

I think of the mime in the Place Pompidou
who gave his balloon to a child; the crowd smiled,
but when he retrieved the balloon it was heavy –

a leaden ball that he couldn't budge.
Each time the girl took it back, it bounced
but the mime strained and grunted;
                                        every ounce
of concentration in that crowd couldn't will
his balloon free.
            . . . Suddenly he released it:
it rose, floated over our heads,
we breathed again, and laughed and cheered.

'Everything's stretching outwards,' you say.
'It's true!' your voice trembled with urgency;
'everything's moving apart, irretrievably.'

Meanwhile the couple behind us hold hands.

There Was a Time

There was a time
when our eyes gleamed across a table
when our words twisted tight around each other's
when your voice in the next room
slipping through the din
could send a shiver through me like a thin wire
stretched tight.

There was a time when the sound of your name
or the sight of your writing
or the thought of you smiling
or the idea that any phone ringing might be you
could make me quiver like a blade flicked out at night.

This evening with a child's toy bulging in your pocket
and the jacket of a pregnant woman
draped across your arm
we laughed, and teased,
and squeezed each other's fingers
and joked about the love affair we never did explore
and both our spouses joked along.

But when they drifted off you broke from me
then lingered, then moved on.
There was a moment, but the time had gone.

Cuckoo's Song

Somehow
however dignified
the cuckold is always a fool.

A difficult role –
I know, I've played it, played the scene:
strutted and fretted,
and finally muttered my way off the stage.

I don't mean to be mean,
but I'd like to see if you've aged
if those fine, high cheeks, that jaw so lean
so honed with contentment
has sagged; and the satisfaction
which seemed a mite smug to us who had none
has gone slightly awry;
and those eyes, so impossibly smooth and true blue,
have become embittered, or at least bewildered
into a murkier hue.

Funny how, however discreet, understanding
however you try not to kick up a fuss
the cuckold is always a wee bit ridiculous.

It isn't the right thing to say
– I never was much good with the lines
and your friends will have used them all anyway –

but somehow, dear Michael,
who seemed to have it all sussed,
I'd like to see if you're still so attractive
now you're one of us.

Only Connect

You're driving along, dreaming of sex with a stranger
you swirl a U-turn;
suddenly two times two tons of metal
crash, as the unseen other
comes barrelling out of the tunnel.

Glass in your throat. You spit
then twist to open the door
it pokes like some elbow out of its socket
sticking up through the skin.
A shower of diamonds cover you;

reaching to brush the bits from your hair
your hand returns red.
You crawl out the passenger side and notice an old dent
rusting brown, flaking like dried blood.

A man appears. Your brain screams:
only connect; screams:
I'msorryI'msorryI'msorry
but you can't seem to form the words.

He doesn't shout: You could have killed me
we could both be dead!
Just: 'Give me your telephone number,' he says
then he disappears.

As you climb back into the car, the shards
like a shattered chandelier, glitter for yards about.
You reach for the buckle and realize that the seatbelt is
        jammed.

It's this –
not the wind rushing in
from the hole where the back used to be

– it's the long drive home
without the seatbelt's familiar, restraining tug
which disturbs you most of all.

You expect the nightmares:
slow-motion repeats
of the other's inexporable approach.

You tell yourself how lucky you are:
had it happened a second sooner . . .
had there been an oncoming car . . .

But your mind is blind, wiped out with the words
which suddenly came up from nowhere:
Only Connect OnlyConnectOnlyConnect.

HTLV-III

Guttersnipe virus
quicksilver quick
killing quick
changing its shape
making us quake
as all the moralists tried to but failed:
Buddha, John Lennon, Mohammed, the Pope
Faith, Love and Hope
pale into nothing beside HTLV-III.
Irony, finding our own promiscuity
finally succeeded in making us pure;
in deed if not thought
we behave as we ought to now
living our lives as our forefathers taught,
not that we care more now
simply we dare no more,
change isn't wrought through a moral conviction
that eunuch imperative threatening Godswrath:
there is nothing to quell the libido
(like death).

Shirley's Place

Oh to be the egg that Shirley breaks each morning 6 a.m. quick smack, slide, pool of giggling butter, sunny side smiling, clean frame of white bubbling to crispiness. 'How you doin' Jake' regular as clockwork 6.02 door whispers open, hash-browns chopped and turned choppedandturned onions stewing suddenly chopped and turned she scoops the whole lot into one cake, warm plate. 6.04 trucks picking up on East 18th, sliced off sizzling griddle, grill's scraped, burned bits slip while the Big Man dips his fork in my yolk oozing, dribbles, eats me, two clean bites, thick slab of white bread sweeps final juices stuffed smotheringly into one big mouth. Mmmm mmmm.

Chelmno

The woods were suddenly cut through with trains.
What happened to those people yesterday?
Silence, only silence now remains.

When someone disappears his neighbour gains.
They say six million didn't disobey.
The woods were humming all night long with trains.

They shuffled down the road, their legs in chains.
They begged for bread and water on the way.
An awkward silence followed their remains.

Their shit and blood and lice clogged up the drains.
And several men were shot who ran away.
The woods were suddenly alive with trains.

A woman took a stone and slit her veins.
Then raised her arms to heaven and seemed to pray.
An eerie silence fell on her remains.

A forest now obliterates the stains.
Though still it's not a place where children play.
The woods have long been emptied of their trains.
Silence, only silence now remains.

Companions

('companion' : *M.E. com: with; panis: bread*)

I do not know how long I have been here.

When they pass through the bread I keep a piece back
All night I caress it, press it and shape it.
By morning it is a man.
After some days I have several companions.

I etch out a board on the floor with pieces of meat from
    the stew.
These are the ground rules:
the lines fade away before the game's over
you have to imagine them there by the end.

When I'm hungry I start with the pawns
then the knights, then the bishops, then kings.
The Queens I keep till the last; last is best.
I do hate to eat them nevertheless . . .

Solitary

The other men use urine
'piss' if you please
though we make an effort to keep it clean –
so much time, so few chances
you grab your dignity where you can –
(the water's too precious to waste);
I fashion mine with sweat
climbing up and down the wall
nine foot by twelve
– twice the size of a small man's coffin –
scraping my chest and forehead
with the daily allotment of paper
till it's broken down enough to mould:
papier maché to make me a woman –
the paper is meant for our arses
you sacrifice what you have to –
at least my woman doesn't stink.

Intimations of Immortality II

All the artists I have fucked around with
fucked up and been fucked up by
all the poets I have screwed
all the actors I have laid
all the writers I have balled
all the scholars I have flayed
all the suckers I have seduced
or have been seduced by through the years
all those wasted days and nights –
how many will remember me
when my name's up in lights?

I flip through small anthologies looking
for the poets from the past –
their faces long since faded
but their names are etched forever;
I read the bylines of old magazines
for all the journalists who had a scoop
and simply needed someone to believe;
I check the credits of new films
for all the actors who were waiting for a break
– the friend of friends or unknown stranger
who would suddenly appreciate their talents.
I have not forgotten.

Isn't it uncanny
how often one encounters people from the past.
Isn't it uncanny how often people simply slip away
the ones one knew most intimately – absolutely –
for a day . . .

If I am ever famous who will see my name
and stop and say: 'So she's made it after all.
And would she remember me?'

Souvenirs

Headlands

Each year the tide comes in faster than you expect;
you find yourself round the farthest headland
looking onto the sea of sand, which has become
while you were picking gooseberries
suddenly a sea again

you're forced to return by the rocks
swirled like wet clay: looking more like waves
than the waves. You cling
between the bristly curtain of pine
and the rising rug of weeds

it's possible, so long as you don't think about it
– you, a fly, skimming granite –
you slide across rough lichen grasping for niches
pulling you to, pushing you from
the jagged wall

you swear, as you have sworn each year before,
this is the last time you take on the headlands;
each year you cling a little tighter
a little less space between you and the air
knees grazing, feet seeking seams
looking not out, not down to the drop

but in, at aeons of igneous
sliding, plate against plate
imperceptibly giving
– even as you cling to it –
over to the sea.

Doppler Effect

It's a tradition: your mother does it every year
and every year, as far as you remember
she's invited you along.

Ignoring the 'Danger: No Trespassing'
you walk across the beach
picking up the railroad where the sand runs into rock.

You climb, hugging the cliff, listening for the whistle
– there are only a few trains now
and they keep no regular schedule.

If one were to come while you were up here
it would be certain death, smashed on the tracks
or, if you jumped
certain death smashed on the rocks . . .
life has so few certainties.

You stride in silence
your mother, not so agile any more
conserves her energy, besides there's nothing to say
on such a glorious morning: sun slithering off waves
glancing off granite.

You remember the first time you realized
that if the train came there was nothing she could do
and several years later . . .
the even greater shock when you understood
that she must have known this and still she invited you.

And still she invites you.
And still you come.

Beach Scene

For decades you clashed
– rocks tossed in a tiny pool
grating away at each other,

finally we escaped
leaving you to bash and scrape
alone;

returning for the summer visit
'His heart,' you whisper
'Her arthritis,' he explains.

We leave you on the beach
and scramble, relieved
over unyielding rock;

opposite the windwrecked island
with its single bonsaied tree
I turn and see

two tiny figures
hand in hand
helping? hindering? each other
stepping stork-like
through the quicksand

a landscape
a still life . . .

La Chapelle

In the wooden chapel at Porte-au-Persil
now defunct, but still much loved
for picnics
and photos through the tiny arched windows

an open book for comments waits
beside the chipped donation plate;
each year we sign, the same each time, leafing back
to make sure our names haven't disappeared.

We play old tunes on the organ – Lennon, Dylan –
hoping some real religio isn't following in our wake;

finally, growing restless for fresh air
or more lively entertainment
we leave, leaving our change on the plate
secure for another season;

our signatures mark a space that grows infinitesimally
each year, in this place which is as near to God
as any of us can believe in.

Belugas

In the flickering glare of the late news
before switching off for the night
suddenly caught by familiar . . . belugas

those vast arctic angels
sailing south, seeking plankton
which thrives where the salt St Lawrence
swirls at a place called

'Tadoussac'
mispronounced by the British reporter
shoring himself ineffectually
from the wind off the water.

Raw-fingered, gripping his mike too close
he discloses:
factory waste spewed by the ton, by the minute
washing up corpses on sandcastle shores
not dolphins, not mammals; they're toxic sites now
and disposed of accordingly.

But here on TV they still swim, grinning greenly
cavorting in close-up, a three-minute item
lodged between hard news and sports
on a slow day –

those innocent singers
returned to my life in this late night
an ocean, a childhood away.
Claiming their brief span of fame.

Souvenirs

The blue house
viewed from the desk of the Tadoussac ferry:
grey water, rocks rimmed white
with spume, and always
the hope of belugas.

We paid a week's wages
to take the new schooner
out to the feeding ground
in the rain, and saw
nothing. Mother scorned:
'In my day . . .' and indeed

driving home that morning
she got a flock of them
frolicking over the bow.
Later, frustration,
a total waste, I thought,
freezing as the low moan
shuddered us over the Saguenay.

Today,
idling in a library
overlooking the Thames,
what I recall is
not the missed belugas
but the blue house:
not waiting,
not anticipating.

The Passion Plant

this is a poem for you Jean
sitting beside the Pacific
pondering – that great Canadian preoccupation –
not who you are, but where you should be

your passion plant
which shrivelled for years on our balcony
after you left
has finally made the adjustment

moving from the big house to this cottage
it was touch and go for a while
but I noticed just now as I watered the pot
it seems to be growing

tendrils creep
in the cracks of the mortar
beside my front door
where no light breaks

this damp gloom
seems to benefit plants
the cyclamen I bought in November
is still in bloom

from my room I hear conversations
passing on the street
the laughter and giggles
even the whispers slip through my window

feet approach up the hill
round the corner
all day I've been waiting
the footsteps retreat

I woke this morning feeling dizzy
thinking of you and of Canada
all that rock and forest
slipping into the States

a man told me the Mohawks are fighting
over gambling rights
he thinks of feathers and tomahawks
I know it's lawyers and writs

I read little bits in the paper
which say Quebec is splitting
where does that leave me
I wonder

at the top of Hampstead village
with your passion plant
about to burst into blossom
perhaps

I've been dizzy all day
did I say that already?
I woke up this morning with the strong sense
that something was going to happen

Poppies

I was hoping there'd be poppies
in the fields along the way.
I don't know why their absence makes me sad;
I used to hate their redness, that pious hint of death,
the war, remembrance services

until I saw them, frail and swaying
in a field of ripened wheat
one afternoon in Normandy
completely unselfconsciously
despite the men who died upon them.

Now I find I seek them out –
that nonchalance, that steak of red
in gutters, ditches, windswept cliffs, on burnt out hills;
they choosed to be, indeed they seem to thrive
in places other flowers couldn't stay alive.

Sometimes a Seagull

Sometimes a seagull
sweeps round the poplars
which mark out the boundary

of your garden through the window.
Sometimes the cry of a seagull slides
through the glass, past your desk with its thesaurus

and that book about containing
anxiety in institutions,
slicing this silence

of words stacked in order
and the hiss of the trees
patrolling your property.

Sometimes a seagull,
miles from the river
slips into this room

where I ask the questions
which you do not answer
though always the note

with my name neatly typed
in black letters, greets me
at the end of each month.

The Storm

Roots
a house's width across
winkled from the earth

with no more effort
than it takes
to rattle a pane of glass

the biggest fall
almost
silently

a rush of leaves
a brushing past
a gentle thud

stranded
slug-like tendrils
wither in the glare of light

roots that anchored generations
can't withstand
exposure:

there are no certainties
not even trees.

Village Church, Anjou

The stone floor of the side door
is worn into a trough
which mirrors all the Gothic arcs
that crown the Christ inside
crowned further by those painfully naive
and precious golden stars
painted in the lapis sky.

The sheer credulity – it makes you want to cry:
the stained glass bleeding streaks of light
across a dusty floor
worn soft by pious knees and faithful feet.
The blind belief in good and bad
behind the grotesque grins and downcast eyes
which all alone support the columns of this place.

And here I sit,
a cynical young traveller in an ancient land
feeling sad, not for a Christ I never knew
but for a faith I never had.

Holland Park

Between the lunchtime clang
of desperately-trying-to-be sleazy, teasing, teenage girls
to Rambo-rivalling, wet-dreaming boys,
and the dusk rustle of cruisers
looking for a fuck or a buck or something
is the unassuming nonchalance of afternoon

when crazies sit quiet by the pond
and drunks and punks and revolutionaries
sulk in corners
and wrinkled women, frail as pollen
waiting for the wind to pick them off
gather to demand their daily sustenance
of mothers with children, and babies in prams;

this is the time and the place of the dispossessed
when everyone's kind to each other
or at least not unkind
when the lavender exudes her soothing perfume
and the geraniums shine their brightest pink
and the peacocks scream for sheer debauchery

and the babies laugh, and the mothers smile
and the old women almost convince themselves
that death will come as softly as the dusk.

August

(*for E.P.C.*)

Crickets sizzle in the dusk
the oaks strike silhouettes
before dissolving.

A cat purrs in your lap
the dogs between us snore and whimper
as we rock on the verandah
charting all the ones who have divorced or died or sired
since we last sat here together.

The piano flashes out its measured beat
against a swish of wings around the lamp
the click of insects zippering grass
the intermittent moan of trains.

Long after Ashkenazy's played his final note
and you and I retreat
the crickets sizzle on.

Belonging

I
I think of her walking
beside the only saint she knew
– that is, St Lawrence, the river –
picking raspberries and roses
which seem to grow together
in the salt smelling sand
by the creosote of railroad tracks
which march hand in hand with the river:

two channels to the heartland
slicing Charlevoix
with its uneasy marriage
of Indian and French
and the English invaders
– of which she was one.

My grandmother wrote poetry
printed in slim volumes:
'. . . something something hills that I love';
there's a plaque to her in the village church
and one to each of her sisters.

II
In small-town Ontario
the women all wear lipstick
and divorcee is another word for whore;
flirting with despair
in the daily round of five and dime
everyone stole kisses
but only the stinky girls were caught.

On Pecker Hill in Irishtown there was no running
    water;
stray dogs, eyes and noses, boys with rubble-studded
    snowballs ran
but water didn't flow that far.
Just because they're poor you have to be especially nice
but no one wants to sit beside the girls from Irishtown.

III
She married an Englishman in the Abbey,
They questioned her schools, she considered it odd;
She signed her vows in Poet's Corner
In the sight of Keats and Shelley, not God.

They dined in Chelsea, danced in Belgravia
Resided in Kensington my dear,
They fell apart on moving to Hampstead
Where does a small-town girl go from here.

IV
You new hea? Who's ya friend?
Hey I jus wonderd if ya was inseprable or what.

In Duchess II newly risen from the ashes
— cops closed it down again; they wasn't let inside —
sleek black girls smile their honey come on,
lights slice you to slivers and there's no place left to sit.
Frenchie, like a black narcissus,
trembles with suspicion, hesitates
a second, then slips into the beat:
I'm over from New Jersey
Lover's mad at me tonight
says I'm the whore of Babylon
just cause I like to dance.
I don't screw 'less I know you
I don't fuck 'less I'm horney
don't make love unless I love you
Get that? Now, you wanna dance?

Later picking grit from the edges of her eyes
— she's been sleeping with the dogs again —
where's it at tonight . . .

V
My mother wants her ashes
scattered over the river at Ile aux Coudres,
my sister wants hers released to the wind
at Cap a l'Aigle.

VI
it's time gentlemen time
time to go home to your wives
it's time ladies time
time to resume your own lives

ding dong bell
the water has run dry
the girl fell in the well
listen to her cry

ladybird ladybird fly away home,
where's it all gone . . .

VII
Today I live in the country
where my grandmother was born

but I still wake in that place
of patchwork hills beneath clouds
that billow in a certain way
that clouds do nowhere else on earth.

Sometimes I wonder if we were the invaders;
three generations of women loved that place . . .
but love doesn't guarantee belonging.